NOW

NOW

Works on Paper 1976-2006

Poetry and Antipoetry

Tom Fallon

Transition Books

NOW – Works on Paper 1976-2006 – Poetry and Antipoetry
Copyright © 2007 Thomas C. Fallon, Jr.

ISBN: 9781597130356

Library of Congress Control Number: 2006932920

Some word forms in NOW have been published in various print and online literary magazines such as the Wisconsin Review, Acorn, Spacebreather, Puckerbrush Review, Le Riviere Revue, Wolf Moon Press Journal, Choomia, Xanadu, Words & Images, The Cafe Review, Animus, etc. The writer is notorious for not submitting work for publication so some of these word forms have never been submitted.

Many have encouraged me along the way: those in the early MWPA; the Maine Arts Commission; Constance Hunting, Margaret Whooley, Lee Sharkey, Mark Melnicove, Gary Lawless, Bern Porter, Patricia Smith Ranzoni, Laurie Meunier Graves, Lisa Saxton, Judith Hakola, George Van Deventer, Linda Tatelbaum, Sandy Phippen.

Printed for Transition Books by
Goose River Press
3400 Friendship Road
Waldoboro Maine 04572-6337

First Edition

For Jacqueline

with whom everything has been created

Urge and urge and urge,
Always the procreant urge of the world.

Walt Whitman, *Song of Myself*

...penetrate to the region of that secret place where primeval power nurtures
all evolution. There, where the powerhouse of all time and space – call it brain or
heart of creation – activates every function; who is the artist who would not
dwell there.... In the womb of nature, at the source of all creation,
where the secret key to all lies guarded.

Paul Klee, *On Modern Art*

What I write, as I have said before, is only called poetry because
there is no other category...

Marianne Moore - Interview with Donald Hall
for the Paris Review

Contents

Introduction: NOW

Now is the time of creation –

Now – the moment – is the time & place of creation – Living time & place is where creative form is
made – As Paul Klee stated – "in the womb of nature, at the source of all creation"– It is simple –
every day – extraordinary in the ordinary way – The simple moment extra-ordinary –

"How should I think?" – as a youth I asked the question when I recognized I did not agree with all the
ideas & values I'd been taught at home & in school – & the question stirred me to write notes
& questions in small pocket notebooks about society, life, myself, etc. – as I sought to understand
how I should live if I could not agree with those ideas & values –

A child of the middle class & popular culture in America – schooled for the American Dream –
I moved to explore the shelves in a small town library to answer the questions – add a talent
for drawing, a desire to be an artist, & I exposed myself to the artists of history, then modern artists,
Cezanne, Van Gogh, Picasso, Dali – the moderns electrifying with free experiment – & free lifestyle –
& I was also exposed to Faulkner's "The Sound and the Fury" non-traditional literary form –

I didn't answer the question how I should live – the small notebooks led nowhere – so I began
to create short works of art in the notebooks to gain something from the writing –
& I was presented with another question – "How should I write?"

Then away from home freely exploring libraries, bookstalls, music stores in NYC, I found Ezra Pound,
T. S. Eliot, e. e. cummings – music John Coltrane, Ravi Shankar – theater Cafe La Mama, Cafe Cino,
Edward Albee, LeRoi Jones, Jean-Claude van Itallie, Sam Shepard, Samuel Beckett –
Judson Memorial Church, Caravan Theater, Theater Company of Boston, Atma Theater Company –
film Ingmar Bergman, Akira Kurosawa & others – & Strindberg, Ibsen, O'Neill –
poetry Hart Crane, William Carlos Williams, Charles Olson, Marianne Moore, Dylan Thomas reading,
the Beats, Nicanor Parra, Dick Higgins, Jackson MacLow – collage, concrete creations, happenings,
chance, found collections – Bern Porter –
Rothko, Pollock, deKooning, Still, Rauschenberg – music Bela Bartok, Edgar Varese, John Cage, Charles
Ives, Thelonius Monk, Ornette Coleman, Cecil Taylor, Anthony Braxton, Harry Partch, Steve Reich –
O'Hara & the New York School – &Whitman – so whatever, moving, whenever, freely moving –

So a simple philosophy of the creative act developed through time – from time – place – from now –

Creation of life springing many different life forms – None, from the creative point of view, superior –
each a creation, a life, a created form, each exists, each acceptable, equal to others – Creation an
experiment, an investigation, what can be created, resulting in innovations, multiplicity of created forms –

We human beings in an age of experiment, investigation & innovations – embracing as exciting
life's creations – The investigation of literary form & diction, experiment, investigation,
resulting in a multiplicity of created literary forms, as natural as the multiplicity of created life forms –
So the source of creation – so the source of creation –

Now – the moment – is the time and place of creation – is "the powerhouse of all time and space" –

Size of this book is due to my necessity for using the space of a page – unfortunately
I cannot use a larger page size than 8 x 10 for the book – so be it –

Tom Fallon

A

The Perfect Machine

off the road

off
the road,
into tall grasses,
wild bushes, ferns
green, dripping
rainwater globules

scooching,
I am surrounded
by green leaves, my head
equal to wild
green bushes

tall grasses and ferns,
pristine water globules
quivering on green leaves
equal to my self

I lay down
in wild green bushes,
tall grasses, ferns green,
water globules
splittering down on
my face

I am
wet and laughing
lying
in wild green bushes,
tall grasses, ferns
green, I am wet,
and laughing

My Funny Valentine

From Miles Davis

Miles and miles ahead
with a piercing cry
from the gold horn.
Black face painted blue,
blue, and bloodied red.

Sound

In the darkness, night,
    from the bed
        I listen
           for the child's breathing,
      turn on the bedside lamp,
              sit on the edge of the bed,
                  look at the child,
          the child sleeping on her stomach,
        hear no sound of the child's breath –

    I watch her back
          for breathing's movement –

              I see no movement, hear
                    no sound, in
                the quiet night –

                    I stand,
              bend over the child's bed,
                bend over the child,
            turning
        my ear to breath,
             listening for sound, and
                    I hear nothing –

             I lift the small child,
        newborn child,
              into my arms, turn her body,
      hold her against me,
          listening for her breath, and I hear
             no sound, feel
            no movement in the child's body –

                  then,
           she moves, and one breath,
                    in and out comes,
    then nothing,
   no movement,
      no sound
        from her –
          I hold the child's body against my body.

                      I hear nothing –

        I listen for her life.

I am in creation

I am in creation –
        I am real –
    I am part of creation –

            I am separate from creation –

        I am flesh and blood –
           I am mind and energy –

       I love life –   I love beauty –
         I love creation –   I love the creator –

I love woman –
          I love the sway
       of a woman's hips walking –

              I love the undulation
                 of woman's Body –
     I desire creation –
          I desire the creator –

       I desire passion –
          I desire the heat of flesh and blood –

       I am flesh and blood, mind and energy, seeking creation –

         I desire
        the flesh and blood,
           the life, the love
            of woman
               in creation –

I desire coupling with a woman physically
        to create another life, to create a new life –

     I desire the juices of creation, the wild passion of sexual coupling –

       I seek the passion of flesh and blood –
          I seek the violence of flesh and blood and love –

              I seek the source of creation actively
                 in the coupling flesh and blood
                   of man and woman –
      I seek the wholeness of creation –

I seek love throbbing and passionate, hot and violent and creative with the juices of life –

       I crucify myself in love's flesh and blood –

I transcend myself in love's violence
to gain creation,
to gain the creator –

I seek the creator, my maker, in love,
in flesh and blood, in creativity,
in the wild juices of life –

I am immortal flesh and blood –

I am a creator –

I live!

The Perfect Machine

From Thelonius Monk

O such a perfect machine!

What is it?
Take it   apart –

one piece   at a time –
Break it down –
one word   at a time   yes –
lay the pieces – the words – on the desk –

NOW –
put it together – create
a new mechanism – change   perfection

to mark time –
to   mark   time –
Ha! I've got it!

TAKE IT A-PART, BROTHER!

(...you will not know, if you do not...)   A p a r t –   S : T : R : E : T : C : H :

Now!   take   it –   take, *it...*   take......it......a-part
a P a r t – !

Girl, in a small town

              now   /   a nice day   Living   not home Patti was - Late
                                         daughter   after school
                    ordinary   -   the unusual   -   today   -   at the library,
   football field   well, she just didn't appear and
                                                        two strangers   / Main Street / beat-up truck
                    Mom, Mary, preparing spaghetti
                                                                 after school .   coming home Patti
   Patti   will be home /   however

                                         not home, Patti did
                    Spaghetti's cold calling girlfriend - No
                                   Mary calling girlfriend - no   no Patti   Patti left
   (not home my daughter)   late, Ted,   Dad?   When -   what -
                                                     and she left Lainie's house two hours
              not home   after school   daughter was not home after school   however
   no call
                                                        truck drifting off Main Street
        Patti left   Patti   will be home, Ted /   however,
              Police   call   Patti left
        not home Patti was -   Late -   Night /   searching and /   missing / searching
                    at the edge of town
                              at the edge of town   *night falling the sun sets*
   (strange truck)   Patti left
          police   combing Hale woods   naturally
                    Patti left   Patti is found and she isn't missing now -
   in a ditch near Hale woods - Patti is found and she isn't missing -
              meet her   strange   girl   *Patti left*
                         / DEAD / RAPED / BEATEN TO DEATH /
                    when cold spaghetti sits on the kitchen table
        driving outta town
                                         "Patti's dead?"   Night And Patti's Not Home
   After School   two strangers driving off Main Street
                         my daughter is dead my daughter is dead my daughter is dead now
              not home my daughter Patti was late and the sun has set -   night   -
   Patti   Patti left   *the car is in the driveway at Olsen's and all*
                                                            in Hale woods
        Was she raped?   We found your daughter, Mr. Olsen /
   strangers   meet   and we think
                    all the lights were on at the Olsen's house   Patti left
              not home Patti was - Late
                    we think   *we must go*   now   *Patti left*
   / DEAD / RAPED / BEATEN TO DEATH /   strangers now
   in a small town   Life
              after school today   meeting   finally
                              - dead   *off Main street -*   *cars - trucks - passing*
        "Patti's dead?"   (now)
                                                        Patti's dead /   raped /
   - where did they go   - where did they come from   Patti's dead   RAPED
                    Patti's not home   Patti's not home

Running Naked

Running naked
through the shading trees of green leaves,
sunlight and shade flashing through
my running mind,
penis flopping in air
against my thighs, running across
the brook, stepping stones

running
up the green tall-grassed hill, running
naked, hitting
the top of the hill, blue sky opening wide
before me, sun white and hot in air
hot on my naked body running,
running down
through green-

tall grass, the sun bright
in the blue sky,
hot on my nakedness,
running faster wind coursing fresh
around my body, running faster down hill
through the green grass racing,
down, down,
penis flopping

free on my naked thighs,
flying down the hill in the sun's heat
the tall green grass thrushing
against my naked legs,
the green grass shushing
in my ears, sun heating my head
and naked shoulders and chest
racing faster and faster
down the hill laughing and
laughing laughing running through the field
past the cows and bull laughing
through the green-tall grass, the sun hot
on my naked body

breathing in the air and racing naked
past the great white pines
laughing, laughing free
my naked mind escaping my naked body,
naked joy
naked glory, naked victory, my naked body
racing racing in the sun's light, penis

                        flopping free, free
              green leaves' shade and light, green
                        grass shushing,
         brook, sun light, open sky, white pines
              wind on my body
                                   flashing through
                        my naked mind,
              running running running
                        naked,
         feeling my nakedness,
              feeling my naked spirit
                             free,
                        free
              free.

Moment

I wake to see white snow heaping dark tree branches

                              with beauty, and I see

                    beauty exploding in the creation of this moment's flower.

~~one black child~~
~~one black child~~
~~one black child~~
~~one black child~~
~~one black child~~
~~one black child~~
~~one black child~~
~~one black child~~
~~one black child~~
~~one black child~~
~~one black child~~
~~one black child~~
~~one black child~~
~~one black child~~
~~one black child~~
~~one black child~~
~~one black child~~
~~one black child~~
~~one black child~~
~~one black child~~
~~one black child~~
~~one black child~~
~~one black child~~
~~one black child~~
~~one black child~~
~~one black child~~
~~one black child~~
~~one black child~~
~~one black child~~

In Atlanta, Georgia, 1981, 29 black children were murdered.

On this first morning

On this first morning
before sun rise.

I wake.

Morning air unmoving
over the dark lake.

Water moving slow,
quiet, breaking
under hemlock.

Stones in clear water.

A bird squeals sweet
in the trees.

Quiet.

Across the lake, dark hemlock.

Clear water moving slow,
quiet, over stones.

On this first morning
at the lake, dark mountain
distant, grey sky
distant.

Water breaking.

Sun rise,

sky bluing,

without sound.

Morning air unmoving.

First lesson

Five years old, Tommy.

The boy running in the twilight
with his younger brother and
girl friend next door.

Mother talking with the neighbor
in the twilight.

Between the Fallon house and
the neighbor's house,
the kids running pell mell,
birds diving
in the darkening air.

Tommy ran nose first into
his brother's head,
stopped,
the crash in his mind.

Blood flowing.

The boy saw death immediately:
he saw his own death.

He saw oblivion.

This was the beginning of God.

The boy knew death.

LIE!

LIE! LIE! LIE!
             (- lie to me PR Man -
with my beautiful language -)

Take my ancient language
      Take my ancient language   Take my ancient language
            and   dis-tort   the Meaning
        of   the   words   -   LIE, LIE,
TO THE PEOPLE!
               cover up/cover up/cover up/cover up/cover up
    the Truth,   cover up   Life   Blind the People to Truth
    Blind the People to Life   *mask the truth of life*
            with your sweet sweet lies PR man, don't,

DON'T UNCOVER THE TRUTH
  PR MAN!   *(- rape the ancient beautiful*
      language of human civilization PR Man -)

GREED! GREED! GREED - PRAY ON
      MAMMON'S ALTAR WITH CURSES
          AGAINST TRUTH OH HOLY
             PORNOGRAPHER OF
    THE HOLY HUMAN LANGUAGE!
        priests of Mammon   PR Man   Con Man
(- straining ideas, distorting love, breaking the Word -)

BREAKING   TRUTH!   *PR Man,*
        lying through your beautiful white capped teeth!
Con Man   Lying
     through your teeth!

WITH THE LANGUAGE OF JOHN DONNE
    WITH THE LANGUAGE OF WILLIAM SHAKESPEARE
    WITH THE LANGUAGE OF EMILY DICKINSON
      WITH THE LANGUAGE OF MARIANNE MOORE

        with,   the language,   *Oh yes,*   OF GERTRUDE STEIN!

O you beautiful graceful liar in Brooks Brothers finest suits /
    mouthing empty words / parroting Mammon / robot of human love

PR WHORE IN THE TEMPLE !   *OUT! OUT! OUT!*

chase the word whores out of the temple
chase the word whores out of the temple chase the word whores out of the temple

Eternal hate campaign of PR men, Smiling Fascists of human language,
Smiling Traitors of human civilization   SMILING TRAITORS OF HUMAN CIVILIZATION

TERRORISTS   OF   OUR

BEAUTIFUL   HUMAN   WORD
SMILE!

LET ME SEE YOUR BEAUTIFUL WHITE CAPPED LYING TEETH!

deadsoul/deadsoul/deadsoul/deadsoul/deadsoul/deadsoul/deadsoul/deadsoul/

YOUR SOUL IS DEAD PR MAN   *your soul is dead pr man*   *LIE LIE LIE LIE*

Snow Fall

Slow,
     snow falls
          to the earth,
                gently.

Slow
          the line of a woman's hip
          moves, flesh
                undulating
                     gently.

Slow,
          a man's painful
          prayer rises,
                releasing his soul
                     gently.

Slow
          a child's clear spittle
                falls
          to mother's cheek,
                gently.

In the silence,
     in the night,
          snow falls,
                gently.

B

In Sight

In Sight Notes

The space and time of words on a page so constructed to create a rhythm probing reality – from the human perspective –

In Sight has slowed the usual time of words on a page with increased space between lines – with single words or short lines – this time natural from my mind's creative rhythm during the work –

Creation is in the body and in the mind and in the society and in the age – as in the universe –

TF

In

one

moment,

point,

in time,

the man

sees;

with faith,

his eyes,

his mind, he

sees

Creation,

immediate,

creation simultaneous,

charged.

The man believes

what

he sees,

Creation

a continuous

time scale,

in one moment,

in space,

physical,

creation immediate,

simultaneous

in

sight.

In

     the early morning

          light,

            on the island,

    the man breathes slowly

and evenly,

     his eyes

   opening,

      rising from sleep

       with the sun rise,

  seeing

    through a window

 in the house,

     the sun;

    seeing the sky

       changing color

    from grey

seeing

  the sun lighting

     the earth;

      seeing green leafed trees

      throwing shade

        on grass,

    on earth,

   in his back field,

hearing the chorus of the birds in the trees;

   hearing

     the sound of the ocean

       hidden

        by the trees.

  In

one moment,

one point,

in time,

this morning,

the man

standing on the porch,

believing

the fresh air in his nostrils,

believing

the morning cool air

on his skin;

believing

the white sun

atop the hill;

believing green leafed trees,

believing shadows on the grass,

believing the sound

of the birds, believing

the sounding

ocean

hidden by the trees,

and

stepping off the porch into the grass

wet with dew,

grass wetting

his bare feet cool,

feeling

the sun warming the air,

warming his skin,

the man believing

Creation,

believing creation

immediate,

simultaneous,

charged

in sight

lifted out of time

now.

In

one

moment,

a point,

in

time,

the man

walking through the grass

in the sun warming air,

the black dog barking

and running through the dew-wet grass

with abandon, the man

laughing and

slapping his knee,

seeing through his eyes,

his mind,

Creation,

receiving creation

with faith

in a moment created

in him self,

powerful,

the Creator creating

now.

In the warm afternoon sun light
on the island,
people coming,
gathering around the man in the grass,
and he speaking quietly to them in poetry
of Creation,

moving
the green leaves of the trees slowly,
shadows moving across the grass,
the sound of the ocean
and
the man
opening his mind
to them,
opening his creation, opening
Creation
in
one
moment
of time,
speaking quietly to them in poetry
of
his Creator,
of his faith,
showing them
a sparrow
in his open hand,
lifting them
out of time
now.

Their eyes and minds opening,

                receiving creation

             immediate,

     Creation,

        in his

           moment

               in side, out side

                    time.

             And they left him,

              filled

                 with creation,

automobiles passing them

       as they walked through the green leafed trees

        laughing and talking,

              free,

          immediate,

        simultaneous,

   receiving

       through creation

            power,

            love

              in Creation

              now.

Shots and laughter rang

       as automobile tires squealed

      on the street,

the sun setting behind the hill,

     clouds aflame

         and the man

           bleeding, dying,

with the sparrow in his open hand,

with faith

in his Creator.

The man disappeared in side Creation.

At

night,

the moon full in the dark sky, round,

people walking

with their eyes and their minds open

to creation,

Creation, open

to

their Creator,

laughing and talking,

in side,

out side,

time,

the black dog barking and running with abandon

through the grass,

the leafed trees lighted white

by the moon.

The people believing the moon and the night.

Clouds passing over the moon

and the trees.

The sparrow is in a tree,

the sound of the ocean hidden

in the trees.

Rain falling slowly, softly, on the trees
    in the night.

        In
            time,
                in side,
                      Creation,
                          creation
                immediate,
                simultaneous,
                  charged
           in
              one
                    moment,
          the point,
              in sight
   origin
       of
          Creation
    in nothing.

The man disappearing in side creation.

    The storm coming in from the ocean, rain
    pouring on wind-tossed trees, pelting
  cemetery headstones
          in the night.

    The sparrow is in a tree.

   (Power;
  love: violence;
      beauty,

     charged;

       creation

         in side, out

         side,

   nothing;

      in

    sight

no thing

   in Creation.)

      The man, John Pierson, died.

       He is buried in the earth.

         He is nothing

         now.

  The rain storm

   stopped.

    Now.

2.

In sight
John Pierson, thin,
a little over five-seven in height,
eyes brown, hair
a lighter shade of brown
and receding from his forehead.
Not handsome
his ears protruding a little too much
and his eyes set too close.
Pierson is not distinctive
looking in any way.
He smiles often.
Sometimes, he feeds a sparrow sitting in his hand.

Pierson is a man of the island. He lives down the road.
He is ordinary.

A washcloth

A washcloth is on the rim
of the sink. It is wet,
pink.

A thin white bar of soap
next to the washcloth.

The faucet dripping slowly
into the sink.

The pink, wet, washcloth
forms a soft mound
with three ridges.

C

Bastard Leaves

Shout Black Mingus, YEAAMEN!

From Charles Mingus

Hallelujah, Black Brother, SHOUT Hallelujah,
                Black Sister! Shout BLACK!
          Black is the color of my skin – ain't no Whitey gonna change my Black Beauty, Lord!

I say SHOUT at Wednesday nite prayer meetin's, shout HALLELUJAH LORD, HALLELUHAH!

        Hallelujah Black Sister, dance, DANCE down
                the aisle – SHOUT Black Beauty, BLACK BEAUTY, the color of my SKIN!

DANCE, DANCE down the streets, Black Brother, SHOUT
      LORD, LORD, ain't no Whitey gonna change my BLACK BEAUTY, We're with you Lord!

     YEAAMEN, HALLELUJAH! Black, BLACK BLACK BLACK! is the color of my beauty, LORD!

        SHOUT IT! SHOUT IT! Dance it!
            YEAAMEN Lord! HALLELUJAH! BLACK, IS THE COLOR OF MY SKIN!

       SHOUT, SHOUT, AND DANCE, THE COLOR OF MY SKIN – BLACK BEAUTY!

Hamlet Action

TOOLS: Hardbound copy of *Hamlet* by William Shakespeare; red, yellow, blue felt marking pens.

SETTING: Public sidewalk, anywhere.

ACTION: Read one line aloud from a randomly picked page of the book and then write or print any
    word that comes to mind on the page with one of the felt pens; tear out the page; drop it to the
    sidewalk; walk away at least ten feet from where you dropped the page.

    Continue these actions until all the pages have been randomly torn from the book.

    Drop the book to the sidewalk and walk away.

The Sacrifice

For the children

The boy was always smiling.

The boy in his room heard
her shout, "Get out," turning the music
louder
but he heard a door slam.

The door opened,
"He's gone. He won't touch you again,"
and the door shut, the music loud
as he stared at the wall from the bed.
Two husbands, he thought.
Now they were alone again,
his face swollen, still warm.
And the door opened, an ice pack
landed on the bed, the door closed.
The boy didn't reach for the ice pack.
The boy pounded his fist
into the baseball glove, slowly,
awkwardly, sitting on the floor, smiling.

"Hey, here comes a real loser now," the older boy nudged
his companion, "Watch."

The boy felt anxiety when
he saw the boys hanging around
in the quadrangle outside school as he approached slowly.
"Woo, watch it boy," the older boy said, leaning toward him,
hitting him with his shoulder.

He jumped away
fearfully, stumbling, falling
to the sidewalk, losing
his baseball glove.
The older boy placed his foot on the fallen boy's chest, laughing.
All the boys laughed.
And the girls laughed.
The boy laughed from the sidewalk.

The boy did not
have a uniform
like the other boys because no uniform would fit him.
He was too small. He had a cap
and he was happy. He did not play in any games,
but he had a baseball cap. He smiled.

He feared them.

"Why can't you perform

in school, you dummy, like other kids,"
his mother asked the boy.
The boy didn't answer
because he didn't know the answer.
He liked school. He liked baseball.

"You're going to study from now on. I'm taking away your trucks
until you get better ranks. You hear," she shouted.

The boy drew a truck on the wall, down beside his bed, out of his mother's sight.

The girls were laughing at his shoes. He smiled at the girls.
He adjusted his baseball cap the way Roger Clemens did.

"I'm afraid he will have to repeat the tenth grade,"
the teacher said.

The boy pounded his fist into the baseball glove,
slowly, awkwardly, standing in front of the mirror.
He adjusted his cap. He smiled.

The boy walked slowly close
to the wall, hoping
the boys wouldn't see him.

The door slammed.

"I'm sorry, but he can't seem to keep up with the others.
I don't think he performs up to his level," the teacher said.

The boy pounded his fist into the baseball glove.
He adjusted his cap the way Roger Clemens did.
He smiled to himself in the mirror. He bent forward,
looking for the catcher's sign. Then he began his windup,
and pitched the ball. He smiled, reached his glove up to receive the ball from the catcher.
He adjusted his cap again. He looked in the mirror and smiled to himself.
He liked baseball.

The boy was always smiling.

The boy repeated the tenth grade.
He studied. He hid his baseball glove
so his mother wouldn't take it.
He colored the truck with red crayon now.
And he was happy.

Get out of here and don't come back you animal she shouted

"He will not
graduate with his class. I'm so sorry.

And he doesn't seem to understand
                what's going on," the teacher said.
          "He seems happy whether
he fails or not. He's still innocent like a child.
                          He just doesn't understand."

The boy adjusted his cap as Roger Clemens did in front of the bathroom mirror.
        He did not smile. He looked at himself.
              He could hear the boys laughing, the girls laughing.
              He folded his arms across his chest, his eyes without emotion
                          in the mirror He was afraid of them.
                  His anxiety rose and he put his hands on the sides of the sink.
                    The sink was cold.
                              His mouth twisted in agony.

        "Woo, watch out there, loser," the older boy said with a smile, hitting
                  the boy hard with his elbow, the boy jumping away with a short laugh,
          falling to the sidewalk, holding his baseball glove to his stomach.

                    The older boy placed his foot on the boy's chest laughing,
                        "Loser," he said, and all the boys laughed.
          The girls laughed at the boy.

The boy lay on his back, smiling.

        When are you going to be like other kids she shouted in his face.
        You'll never go to college like other kids you dummy she shouted in his face.

          Lying on the sidewalk, the boy laughing over him,
                    the boys and girls laughing at him,
              he took the pistol slowly from his baseball glove and shot the boy
                                    in the face.

                    The boys and girls ran, screaming.

        He shot the pistol three more times and killed another boy and a girl.

The boy lay on the sidewalk in the quadrangle, a dead boy at his side. He raised the pistol in the air
                            as if in victory. He was smiling.

                  The quadrangle was quiet
          when the police sharpshooter shot the boy.

        "The kid's smiling," a policeman said, standing over the dead boy.
            "What the hell," he said with an awkward laugh
                  as he kicked the baseball glove away.

                        A young priest knelt over the boy
                        and made the sign of the cross.

Blood stained the sidewalk.

GM morning television news broadcast the story live around the world
to civilized and primitive societies
from the well-manicured school quadrangle in the affluent American city.

The GM woman reporter held her microphone up
to a boy's face:
"He wasn't like the rest of us.
He was alone a lot. He was kinda weird, smiling all the time.
You know, like a crazy. I don't know. He's dead now.
It's over, I guess."

A black Lincoln Continental stopped at the school.
The city's mayor walked up the sidewalk to the quadrangle
where the three boys and girl had died and set down a white floral wreath.
He bowed his head for a moment, then returned to the car.

The GM news broadcast featured the mayor setting down the floral wreath
on the evening news.

The morning after the killings, the blood stained quadrangle was filled with white flowers, teddy bears and
poems, students and parents praying and crying.

The GM television camera zoomed to the tear stained human faces.

Three days later school was in session and the quadrangle
was milling with boys and girls talking and laughing,
the boys playing football with a teddy bear.

The white flowers wilted and turned brown in the sunlight.

The GM television camera zoomed to the brown flower petals

The boy, Tim Lenden,
was dead.

Jim Carson, Milty Hewitt and Louanne Meyer were dead.

The janitor swept the brown flower petals
into a garbage bag.

Before

I was conceived, I did not hear the music on the radio.
I did not hear my mother's voice.

From Marin's hand

no stone   / granite   – no granite

with Marin   / from   BUT THERE IS

the ocean
dissociated   / the land without moorings

EARTH   /
broken   /   UNREAL
nothing   here   realized   /

washed out colors from Marin's hand & MIND   /
& mind   / & mind   /

Deer Isle   – destroyed

on paper,
in Amerika

WHAT   DOES   THIS   MEAN

up in the air   / *is there nothing solid in the water*

an island   /   in flight   /
where?

Brown   Blue   Green   White   black   / here

Deer Isle, Maine 1921 - Watercolor and charcoal on paper, 14" by 17', John Marin

The Peach

The flavor of a peach, ripe,
swollen with juice, orange
with red blush, round, round,
and furred soft, is like a
woman –
ripe, juice squirting
in my eye, overflowing my mouth
and dripping down my chin.
Oh, the ripe fruit, oh the
peach, the full flavored juice!
Oh the round peach, yes!
Yes!

Ghost Dance

Snow,
 cold, white, blowing
   wild
 and freezing the natives
   in ugly postures of
                death –
         bullet-riddled bodies
       of Lakotas frozen
           in white snow,
 the Sergeant remembered in the dark,
     sweating
           in the dark –

The natives corralled
   in a hollow, Wounded Knee,
       gathered around Chief Big Foot,
     heading to the Badlands
         for the Ghost Dance,
       surrendering peacefully
       to the Seventh Cavalry
           December 28th,
   the man remembered in the dark, sweating,
       holding the Bible in his hand –

Cold,
   the snow
     at Wounded Knee,
 drifting over men, drifting over women, drifting
   over children
         dead,
           bullet-riddled bodies
       of the Lakotas frozen to
                 white earth –
   the Seventh Cavalry surrounding
     the natives, automatic Hotchkiss guns
       trained on the Lakotas gathered
       together against the cold,
         small fires in the night,
           huddled around Chief Big Foot,
   the man saw, alone in the dark,
           his Bible in hand,
       listening to the rattling breath
               of sleeping men
             in the barracks –

Snow,
   cold, white, blowing
       wild

and freezing the natives
   in ugly postures of
                  death —
        bullet-riddled bodies
     of Lakotas frozen
          in white snow,
the man turned over in his bunk, pressing
the Bible to his chest, closing his eyes
       against the vision —

Soldiers of the Seventh Cavalry digging
   at the frozen earth, cutting a rectangular hole,
    bodies of natives piled
          in a buckboard frozen, frozen,
      he and another soldier dragging a grotesque
frozen woman's body, standing her up,
      grabbing her between the legs
         and sliding her into the buckboard
      over dead Lakotas,
         he and the soldier laughing,
   shouting at the piled human beings
     "Dance, ghost, dance! Ha ha, ha ha!"
    moving in native dance fashion,
              "Dance, ghost!
              Hoo hoo, hoo hooo!"
Cold,
   the snow
     at Wounded Knee,
drifting over men, drifting over women, drifting
   over children
       dead,
        bullet-riddled bodies
     of the Lakotas frozen to the
            white earth —
the Sergeant opened his eyes to clear the vision
      of death,
   clutching his Bible, sweating, shivering
in the dark, listening to the rattling breath
        of sleeping men in the dark —

The soldier
   kicked at a child frozen to the earth,
    kicking the dead child and cursing,
     dragging the small deformed human
        to the rectangular hole, swinging the body
    around in the air and
     into the grave of piled frozen
             Lakotas,

laughing, shouting, "Dance, Wovoka, Dance!
Ha ha ha ha" dancing
in the dark, human voices –

A man
cutting, tearing a Ghost Shirt savagely
from a frozen brave,
himself dancing
in the Ghost Shirt, shouting, "Ghost Shirts don't
work! Ghost Shirts don't work!
Hoo hoo, hoo hooo!"

Snow,
cold, white, blowing
wild
and freezing the natives
in ugly postures of
death –
bullet-riddled bodies
of Lakotas frozen
in white snow,
the rattling breath of sleeping men
in the Sergeant's ears –

The man sat on the edge of the bunk in the dark,
staring at mounds of sleeping human beings,
and sweating, shivering,
he slid on his boots,
pulled a blanket round quaking shoulders,
scuffed between the bunks
holding the Bible to his chest,
opened the door to frozen air,
stepped into white snow, stepped down
snow drifted steps, snow wild
in the howling wind,
seeing
unarmed natives in the hollow
surrounded by the Seventh Cavalry with automatic
Hotchkiss guns, the rattling
of guns, natives screaming,
natives scattering,
falling, men, women and
children
running, screaming, automatic guns rattling,
children screaming, falling,
the natives running in every direction,
automatic guns rattling, rattling, rattling, screaming
children running wild –

The man
trudged slowly through the deep snow
in the fort compound,
wind freezing him with snow,
dropping the Bible, moving toward the flagless
pole
piercing the white sky
over head

seeing
human body
of Chief Big Foot,
frozen,
dead, ugly,
swung by two soldiers
into the grave on top of frozen Lakotas,
dead men,
dead women,
dead children
snow
flailing the man, freezing he felt nothing,
remembered nothing
at the foot
of the flagpole.

Brother soldiers found the man
next morning
frozen,
ugly,
in the posture of death.

The man's Bible in the snow, frozen.

"Bury him,"
the colonel said.

The flagpole,
without flag,
pierced
the frozen,
sunlighted,
blue sky.

Sugar Song

From Frank Sinatra

The smooth silk voice
makes you feel so good.
Life is white, white
with a sugar-dripping-song.

Tenderly

From Ben Webster

In the soft light, slowly peeling
away the layers of the pain,
leaving her naked in the air,
leaving her without her skin.

Solo

From Judy Garland

Her voice rising in song,
quavering in its flight,
beauty with uncertainty:
her throat tearing.

Mary Hanged

The museum was immaculate   white and well-lighted,
        the exhibits carefully arranged   behind glass
                costumes white

And the young brown-skinned woman   Jawanna   explaining to the tourists
        the white costumes   worn by the Ku Klux Klan,
                and the wooden cross   the noose for lynching,
                        for death

And the young brown-skinned woman rested   after the tourists left
        sitting under the mural   of a lynching,
        a black man hanging from a tree   in a cotton field,
                Klan members gathered around the tree   talking and smoking,
        Jawanna   with a restrained smile fixed on her lips

White ghosts   the young woman Jawanna thought
        she knew the story   from her grandmother
                at her knee Sunday   after church
                the white ghosts came   in the sweltering night
                        marching, shouting   shouting, enraged

And the nigger Mary Turner   challenging
        her husband lynched   I'll take them to court
        Mary promising   eight months pregnant
                sending a shock of fear   through her people

And the white ghosts came in the night   with the wooden cross
        the Ku Klux Klan burning the cross   at Mary Turner's door
in the cotton field   enraged by the nigger's defiance

And white women and children that night   havin' a good time, they were
        her grandmother said   roun' that burnin' cross

And the Ku Klux Klan torched   Mary's cabin
flushing the pregnant woman   Mary ran through the cotton field
                to save her baby's life

She couldn't get away, Poor Mary   Gramma said
        the Klan burnin' the house down   roun' her

And the ghosts caught Mary   the ghosts they beat her
        they tied her legs   draggin' her to a tree
                        pregnant like that
white women an' children kickin' her,   kickin' her, they were

                And the ghosts strung her up   Mary Turner
        Mary she was upside down   from the tree

An' they sliced her stomach open   yes they did, child

They cut that baby right outta her
and they crushed that unborn baby's head down in the dirt   they did, like animals
                              cross burnin' in the cotton field

An' they shot her   an' they shot her   they jus' went mad shootin'
     they run outta bullets, those white men   they shot Mary Turner like that

                         They jus' went mad   them white ghosts
             an' that was the way our Mary died   like that, like that

White ghosts   the young brown-skinned woman Jawanna thought
          Ghosts, white ghosts   phantoms they were   the dead

A family of white-skinned tourists entered the immaculate museum
          a young man and a woman, a boy   stopped at the Ku Klux Klan costumes
                    pure white   behind glass

"Good afternoon"   Jawanna said   "Welcome to Georgia's Mary Turner Memorial Museum"
     she said quietly   with a restrained smile.

"The white costumes behind glass"   "You are looking at"
     "Were worn by members"   "of the Ku Klux Klan"
          she said pleasantly   to the white tourists

"That's just like halloween"   the boy blurted out

          "Yes, they were white ghosts"   Jawanna said   "white ghosts"
     "However"   "They were not exactly halloween ghosts, young man"
     "This is what they did"   she said pleasantly
          pointing to the middle of the room   occupied by a tree
     a woman hanging upside down from a limb   her head a foot from the floor
                         her stomach sliced wide open

               "This is Mary"   "Mary Turner"
     The young woman said quietly   lowering her eyes

"Gary, Mother, stand over there, by the tree"   the man said raising his camera
          "That's it. Now smile"   the camera flashed
                         Jawanna was silent
          Then Jawanna said   "This is Mary's child"
               pointing to the child   on the floor
     in the dirt   under Mary's head hanging   the child's head crushed

"Ah, okay, okay, we've seen enough here, I guess"   "Let's go"   the man said

"We've got to make some time"   "Before sundown"   the man said
          "We have to be at Disneyland tomorrow"   "By noon"

                              And the tourists left

The young brown-skinned woman walked back to her seat   under the mural of the lynching
          to wait for more visitors   for more tourists

          The museum was immaculate   white   and well-lighted

          The exhibits were carefully arranged

          Jawanna sitting   with a restrained smile fixing her lips   waiting

Abstraction: Blue life

From Georgia O'Keeffe

                    In the purity and
                                        line
          there is a fullness, a humaness
                                        clearly
                                        made,
               majestic yet
                         intimate, personal,
                    her touch
                              on my hand
                    finger light
                              opening me
               with her trust
                              in the closeness of her flowering,
          yet space sweeping
                    free
                              inside the flower, and living blue,
                                        moist, human,
     a warmth there in her space
                    "a very beautiful world there"
                              wherein the desert morning is
               swelling, flowering,
                         a bloom

Bastard Leaves

1.

& in
Washington, D C,
American,
Walt Whitman

Leaves
made

3rd floor room,
bedpot full,
unmade bed,
half-dressed
at 10 A.M.,
1863

nursing Civil War wounded
soldiers, gangrene

man
offered bread
cut
with pocket knife,
toasted on
stick,
butter,
plate brown paper

tea
brewed in tin cup, sugar
from paper sack

"Sister Hannah
sick & depressed
in Vermont,
Jesse helpless
as Eddy menaced Mother
with a chair"
poet said

"Andrew's dying, TB
& drink, wife
Nancy drinking, pregnant,
ignoring the kids

"Mother & family together

in basement room,
fighting the other tenants"
the man said

nursing Civil War soldiers
Whitman 45, near collapse, depressed,
insomnia, dizzy spells,
headaches,
trembling,
photophobia, deafness,
ear buzz & hum

*nursing war sick & dying, amputees, gangrene ooze on lips, the dead
boy wasting away*

"my brother George's a POW"

poet a clerk
at Indian Affairs
office
"in at 9 if I want,
maybe stay 'til 4"
Whitman said

fired for *Leaves*
at 46

"set out to find George listed a casualty,
tramping the camps, robbed, hunting hospitals, found him OK
at Fredericksburg, a heap of arms & legs in front of his tent

"Andrew died, Jesse took
a fit,
I committed him,
Nancy a prostitute,
War over, many, many boys died"
man said
emptying his bedpot

2.

& in Camden, N J,
328 Mickle St.,
working class neighborhood,
bearded old Whitman in rattan chair,
wolf skin over the back,
writing letters

                    "now a month
            I've been confined to room & bed,
          hot weather, brain & stomach trouble,
            paralytic attack over 4 weeks ago,
              no action at all of bowels
                  or water works"

                  breezes wafting
            fertilizer processing plant
                  man writing

              "baffling cerebral affection,
          grave lesions of the stomach & liver,
          walk very little (I'm crippled, left leg)

        "down again with muscular & nervous prostration,
                  I don't go out much,
        the effect of the sunstroke shocks lingering on"
                    the poet wrote

                  "good bowel action,
              ate egg & tea & bread
                  for breakfast"

            Camden & Amboy trains
                  rattle by
            "an increasing prostration
of the whole muscular system, connected somehow with head derangement,
    almost a falling sickness, at times I can't stand on my legs"

          white bearded old poet in rattan chair
                wolf skin over the back,
                factory whistles blowing,
                    writing letters

            "sick yet with the grip, dark,
            rainy day, still under the bad
                influence of the grip

        "have a dull head ache & eternal inertia,
            am feeling fairly, hot weather,
              the sweat oozes out of me,
            a good normal bowel voidance
                    yesterday,
              another today, good"

                  breezes wafting
            fertilizer processing plant
                old Whitman writing
        from front upstairs room at Mickle St, Jersey

"been scribbling on my final version
of *Leaves* – shall probably
get out in wheel chair presently,
fair bowel action,
I live here 72 years old & completely paralyzed,
brain & right arm about the same,
sight & hearing half-and-half,
spirits fair,
locomotive power almost utterly gone

"have supper at 4:30,
no dinner,
fair excretion business,
out in wheelchair last evening,
my grip has called in upon me again the last two or three days,
(probably the great change in the weather & stoppage of sweating)
not so bad as before"

Methodist Church bells hurt old man's ears &
fife & drum brigade

old poet writing letters
"weak & restless,
real bad bladder trouble interferes with sleep at night,
sit here alone in the big chair this cool weather
big wolfskin spread over myself
against drafts,
bad days & nights, every hour I suffer"

factory whistles blowing
tomb waiting at Harliegh Cemetery

"inveterate inertia & bladder troubles,
I'm deadly weak,
bowel drain sufficient,
growing weaker"

"bowel movement an hour ago,
steady pain in my left side,
propped up in bed,
deadly weak but spark of life still there"
Camden & Amboy trains
rattle by

Walt Whitman wrote
"feeble & weak & restless,
bowel movement every day"

white bearded old man in a rattan chair,
wolf skin over his back, wrote
"Hannah, unable to write much,

"$4 enclosed
your good letter received"

breezes wafting fertilizer from processing plant
Camden & Amboy trains rattle by
old poet stopped writing March 26th, dead

lab worker at the American Anthropometric Society accidentally dropped Whitman's brain
on the floor, destroying it

The poet reading

Last month, I was privileged
to read my poetry at the University;
however, it was an embarrassment
for Our Literature.

Police had to arrest a young woman
for Conduct Unbecoming a Poetry Lover.

You see, the woman danced wildly
as I read, screaming like a banshee,
and she threw her red silk panties at me.

I was appalled. It was humiliating.

It was such a nerve-shattering experience,
I needed an extra valium after the reading.

I still have her red silk panties.

The Visitor

For Bud Powell,
in the asylum

There,

he had drawn the piano

keys

on the wall
and,

banging his fingers against the piano
keys
on the wall
asked
his Visitor, listen

what do you think,
what do you think

of these chords,
what,

banging his fingers on the wall

do
you
think

of, banging his fingers

these chords,
these chords

what,

what,

banging

his fingers on the wall

D

The Arena

Arena Notes

A Catholic church in the small town of Rumford, Maine.

The Arena Chapel, Santa Maria della Carita, in Padua, Italy, is decorated
with the murals of Giotto, painted around 1302, which depict the life of
Jesus Christ. As a young person, I was entranced by these murals and those
of other Renaissance artists who illustrated the life of Christ. And as a man,
I am struck by the stained glass windows in the above named Rumford
church.

I was first introduced to Jesus Christ, and God, religion, by the Renaissance
muralists. I felt that the arena of life, the battleground in the human soul,
which takes place in the universe, in creation, was expressed in the murals.
This art, in my mind, connected to the reality of creation, the creative act.

The Arena is unfinished.

TF

The Arena

The sun shone through
the stained glass window
over the Altar.

The colors were brilliant.

The Church almost empty
for morning Mass.

I genuflected beside the pew.

The stained glass window:
Jesus baptized at the Jordan
by John the Baptist,
a dove descending on Him.

I kneeled in the pew to pray.

I did not pray.

The candles were lit
on the Altar.

The Church was dark.

In silence.

I looked at the baptism
of Jesus, with John,
at the river.

Jesus beginning, I thought,
seeing the brilliant colors
of the stained glass window.

I am here, I thought,
*in Church, to revere God,
and His Son, Jesus.*

I sat back in the pew.

Seven other people were in church.

I thought.

*The fresco of Giotto;
the lamentation over Jesus
in the Arena Chapel.*

*Santa Maria della Carita,
Padua, Italy.*

The candles on the Altar
flickered, danced,
in the silence.

I was quiet.

*Jesus lying in His Mother's
arms, down from the cross,
as Giotto painted.*

*Gold haloes of Jesus,
of Mary, the mourners.*

At Golgotha.

*The chapel walls adorned
with the frescoes of
the Holy Families.*

Margaret walked
slowly down the aisle
with a rosary in her hand.

Light yellow slacks.

I turned away from her
presence.

She stopped at the pew,
stood still. Her slacks
hugged her hips.

Tim walked slowly
with cane down the aisle,
bowed, sat slowly in a pew.

She sat in the pew, kneeled.

A voice came from the sacristy
and Mrs. Arsenault struggled
down the stairs.

She bowed at the Tabernacle.

The Church was quiet.

I thought.

*Giotto had painted the angels
agitated by the crucifixion,
the death of Jesus.*

But the mural was not agitated.

*The form of the human beings
was serene.*

*Young, Margaret is, and I know
she is a virgin. Her form
a perfection.*

I closed my eyes.

In my mind.

*The forms Giotto created
perfect, Jesus held
by His Mother, serene.*

Art for God.

Her form returned. The art
of her living form,
perfect.

Margaret's hair flowered
to her shoulders,
to her white blouse.

She kneeled in the pew
saying the rosary.

Beauty like no other.

The candles on the Altar
flickered, danced,
in the silence.

*The serenity of form Jesus dead,
Mary, the mourners, around Him,
beauty, like no other.*

I kneeled again.

*The story of God on the walls
of the Arena Chapel.*

The candles on the Altar
flickered.

I looked at the baptism
of Jesus, with John,
at the river, over the altar.

The stained glass window
shone beautiful with the sun light.

The colors were brilliant.

Jesus head bowed to God.

Her form. Bloom. Of God.

I thought in the quiet,
in the dark.

In the Church.

The man who loved God,
loved all human beings,
from the beginning,
baptized with water.

In the end, Jesus crucified,
the blood on the earth
of the lover of God.

Giotto painted the lamentation.

Gold haloes of Jesus,
of Mary, the mourners.

I tried to pray.

In my mind.

Forms perfect, beauty,
love, created,
like no other.

Peace with God.

She is beautiful.

I bowed my head
in the Church.

Yellow.

I thought: *There is*
perfect form.

The Church was dark.

I closed my eyes.

Her hair flows.

I opened my eyes,
looked at her, praying.

The sun light shone through
the stained glass window
over the Altar.

The colors brilliant.

A dove descended.

The spirit of God.

Yellow.

I was not quiet.

Giotto painted.

Jesus crucified; dead;
down from the cross;
in Mary's arms.

With Mary Magdalene,
beloved John, Nicodemus,
Joseph of Arimethea.

At Golgotha, Jesus, the son,
with life from God,
crucified.

Santa Maria della Carita,
Padua, Italy.

The candles on the Altar
flickered yellow flame.

I bowed my head.

My heart beating.

"...this is my Beloved Son,
in Whom I am well pleased..."

I raised my head
to the stained glass window,
colors brilliant with sun light.

She is a virgin.

I am here, I thought,
in Church, to revere God,
and His Son, Jesus.

Love...

I bowed my head,
for the love of God.

2 - The Kiss

I sat in the car
with the windows open
in front of the Church.

It was warm,
a late fall morning.

Thinking.

*The frescoes of Mary's life
in the Arena Chapel. Her mother,
and father, Anna and Joachim.*

*Their kiss at the Golden Gate.
Full lips, Giotto painted,
not idealized, human.*

Their bodily fullness.

*Her robe orange, a warm color.
His blue and red. Blue for
ideals, intellect; red for heat,
sexual?*

*A human kiss between a man
and a woman.*

*Not the kiss of Judas. Not
the kiss of a father or
mother for their child.*

*Anna is pregnant. After
being childless, without
new life in her womb.*

*The life of God in creation
has entered her body.*

*The life of a man has entered
the body of the woman.*

The creation, zygote exploding.

*Mary, the Mother of God,
has been conceived
in her mother's womb.*

Miracle.

*The kiss an intimate moment
for a man and his wife.*

As is the conception of a child.

I shouldn't be waiting here.

Waiting for her. For Margaret.

The drawing pad was in my lap.

The radio was playing Baroque
and Renaissance sacred
and secular music.

The blue sky spreading before me.

The Church was on a hill
overlooking the town.

I sat in the car on the hill,
in the shadow
of the Church steeples.

The woods beside me bloomed
in the beautiful red, yellow,
orange and lime leaves of fall.

Behind the Church were dark
white pines reaching high
into the blue sky.

The sun was shining.

*Margaret is not much younger
than I am,* I thought.

I reached for the key in the ignition
to leave.

Margaret came out of church
with Tim.

I didn't turn the key.

Tim moved slowly
down the stairs leaning
on his cane to support himself.

He had lost his lower leg
to diabetes two years ago,
a year after his wife had died.

She was speaking to him

as he moved, her hand reaching
in the air as it to steady him.

I watched her as she came
down the stairs.

Her light yellow slacks hugging
her hips, her white blouse
fitting her small breasts.

Her dark hair flowered
to her shoulders.

Perfect form, I thought.
I could feel the form.
I could feel her form.

She was a vision
in the morning sun light.

They stopped on the sidewalk,
speaking.
She laughed, and he laughed.

She raised a hand to him
and turned away, walking
away down the sidewalk.

I watched her walk.

She is beautiful. Living.

So it is God creates a woman,
I thought. *Beauty here*
on this earth.

She is a virgin. Untouched;
uninvaded; unsullied;
by man. Innocent.

More beautiful than
her body form, her
innocence. More precious.

Her virginity; her beauty.
Purity.

But there is the lure
of her beauty, lure to join
her beauty, put on her beauty.

I would dispel my imperfection,
my sin, my weakness, with
her perfection. Purity.

*Her life giving innocence
and beauty.*

*Body perfect; soul
perfect.*

*To commune with her
in the human way.
Real. Creation way.*

Intimately.

I looked at the sky spreading
before me pure blue.

*Such perfection of form
in the Giotto fresco, created
with such perfect design.*

*God created the beauty
of this world, this miracle
of creation.*

I began to draw on the pad
seeing her form.

*Her light yellow slacks
hugging her hips, her
white blouse fitting
her small breasts.*

*Her dark hair flowering
to her shoulders.*

*The lines of Giotto came
to mind, the composition
of the fresco; form.*

I saw the brilliant colors
of the leaves beside the car,
sun shining in the sky.

A bird spirited across the street.

Two kids were passing a football
in the side street by the church.
They were shouting.

*I could see her naked. beautiful,
as created by God. Art form
as no other, living.*

*A softness created like no other
for human intimacy.*

She was more than pure beauty
for me. She was sexual
I knew. Human.

A fullness.

She was moving farther away.

Her innocence, purity,
virginity, luring me.

To intimate communion.

The fiery red of the maple tree
came into sight as my vision
of her blurred in my thought.

The kiss of Joachim and Anna
 at the Golden Gate.
Lips full, Giotto painted.

Their bodily fullness.

Gold haloes of the holy family

A human kiss between a man
and a woman.

Margaret would sense my desire
if I spoke to her. I could sense
the desire real.

Anna was pregnant with Mary.

Watching Margaret walk away.

Beauty. From the human mind.
In creation.

"And Joachim begat
the Virgin Mary," (from Voragine).
The living child.

Communion creation; sexual
communion; life's genesis.
Joachim and Anna together.

Giotto painted full human lips.
Sensuality of the human.

I thought.

Margaret was far down the street.

"Thus Anna thy wife will bear
thee a daughter, and thou shalt
call her name Mary,"
the Lord's Angel said to Joachim.

"In accordance with your vows
she shall be consecrated to the Lord
from her infancy.

"She will herself beget the Son
of the Most High Whose name
will be called Jesus,
and through Whom salvation
shall come to all nations."

So Voraigne had written.

*The kiss painted by Giotto
in the Arena Chapel.*

A chipmunk scampered
across the street, tail in the air.

Margaret had disappeared.

I turned the key in the ignition,
passing the colored leaves.

*Giotto painted the kiss
of a man and a woman, with
full human lips.*

We were running naked in the woods.

*Mary was born, the Mother
of God.*

I stopped at the school,
looking down the street
where Margaret had walked.

What was I doing?

*I love beauty. I love
creation.*

*Why is this love temptation?
The virgin, a temptation?*

*Why, God?
I do not understand!
Why love is temptation
also.*

3 - Communion

1.

I come to God this afternoon.

I come to Church.

Come,
to this Holy Place.

I made the Sign of the Cross
on myself with Holy Water.

I walk slowly
from the Sacristy
in to the Church.

With humility,
for this
is the place of God.

The Church is empty.

Dark.

The Sanctuary candle burning over
the Tabernacle.

I bend, touch my knee to the floor
before the Tabernacle
which contains the Eucharist.

Where Jesus Christ,
the Son of God,
exists.

I bow my head.

I know I should not be here, God.
I am a sinner.   Forgive me.

I enter the first pew
before the Tabernacle
and kneel.

I am alone.

The Church is in silence.

The sun shines through
the stained glass window
over the Altar.

The colors are brilliant.

The stained glass window of
Jesus baptized at the Jordan
by John the Baptist,
a dove descending on him.

The next window of Jesus
speaking to the Apostles.

And the other window is of John
before the King and Salome.

The stained glass windows by
S. A. Maumejean Freres,
Hendave Paris.

The windows illustrating
Jesus' life are beautiful.

*I am in the Holy Place
of God.*

*The voice of God: "my son
with whom I am pleased."*

*Jesus, head bowed, to John.
And the dove descending on Him.*

I raise my eyes to the Tabernacle
in the silence.

In the darkness.

Jesus is in the tabernacle.

I try not to think my own thoughts.

I believe in God, I think.

*I trust in God, creator.
Author of the creation.*

*I trust.
In God
Who created me.*

*I have seen the world, creation.
I have seen the creation of God.*

I have seen the miracle of creation.

I know God.

God is miraculous.

My life is a miracle.

God is with me.

Not only in Church here.
Every day.
Every ordinary day.

Like the sun rises every day.
Simply, there. Here.

I can talk to Him. I do
talk to Him.
As I would talk to another person.

I cannot see Him, no.
But I do know I can talk to Him.
I do talk to Him.

I do receive answers from Him.
But not in human speech.

In an ordinary, unspectacular way,
as if it were ordinary human speech.

And in silence.

I am in His World.

God is close to me, not distant.
When I speak to Him
I acknowledge His power, His place,
as a simple fact, not with pious
reverence, but with natural reverence.

I have to be humble naturally.

When I ask for His help,
I do not know if I will receive it.
I believe I can receive it
if He wishes.

I believe.

Here, in church, it is different.
Here, in this Holy Place.

With Jesus.

The Son of God came to us.

The God who created the World.
The creation.

Came
to love. To serve.
For love is serving.

I stopped thinking,
bowing my head.

In the silence.

2.

I turned
to the stained glass windows
along the side walls of the Church,
lit by the afternoon sun.

I walked slowly to
the first window in the silence.

The Annunciation to Mary
of her Virgin Birth.
The Angel from God speaking
that she would be the Mother
of our Savior.

God become man.

I closed my eyes
but saw the Annunciation
still.

I opened the Holy Bible
to the word of God.

I made the Sign of the Cross
and whispered in the silence:

"The Angel Gabriel was sent
from God to a town of Galilee
called Nazareth, to a virgin
betrothed to a man named Joseph.
And coming to her He said:
The Holy Spirit will come upon you
and the power of the Most High
will overshadow you. Therefore
the child to be born will be called Holy,
the Son of God."

I walked slowly to
the second window
blazing with color.

*I follow in the footsteps
of Jesus.*

This window is the Birth
of Jesus. With Mary, Joseph,
the baby Jesus,
in the stable.

*I believe in Jesus Christ,
the only begotten Son of God.*

I bowed my head in reverence
to the Lord.

I opened the Holy Bible,
made the Sign of the Cross on myself,
and whispered in the silence:

"And Joseph too went up from Galilee,
from the town of Nazareth to Judea,
to the city of David that is called Bethlehem,
to be enrolled with Mary, his betrothed,
who was with child. While they were there,
the time came for her to have her child;
and she gave birth to her first born son.
She wrapped him in swaddling clothes
and laid him in a manger, because
there was no room for them in the inn."

I walked to the third window
which showed the Presentation
of Jesus in the temple

I believe Jesus is the son of God.

I bowed my head.

I opened the Holy Bible
to the word of God.

I made the Sign of the Cross
on myself and whispered:

"When the days were completed
for their purification, according to
the law of Moses, they took Him
up to Jerusalem to present Him
to the Lord, just as it is written
in the law of the Lord, 'Every male
that opens the womb
shall be consecrated to the Lord,
and to offer the sacrifice
of two turtledoves or two young pigeons,'
in accordance with the dictate
of the law of the Lord."

I walked slowly to the fourth window
of the young Jesus in the Temple
Debating with the Elders

I believe Jesus: I believe.

I believe in God the Creator.

I bowed my head in reverence
to Jesus.

I opened the Holy Bible,
made the Sign of the Cross on myself,
and whispered in the silence:

"When Jesus was twelve years old
his parents went to Jerusalem
for the Passover, as was the custom.
When Mary and Joseph left Jerusalem
for Nazareth after Passover, they lost
Jesus. They returned and found him
after three days in the Temple,
sitting in the midst of the teachers,
listening to them and asking them
questions. And all who heard Him
were astounded at His answers
and His understanding."

The fifth window is Jesus
with the children
at his knees.

I opened the Holy Bible,
made the Sign of the Cross on myself,
and whispered the Word of God:

"Let the children come to me
and do not prevent them;
for the kingdom of God belongs
to such as these. I say who does not
accept the kingdom of God
like a child will not enter it."

I believe in God. I believe.

The sixth window presented
Jesus Preaching the Sermon
on the Mount.

I read the Word of God to myself:

"Love your enemies, do good
to those who hate you, bless
those who curse you, pray
for those who mistreat you."

"To the person who strikes you
on the cheek, offer the other one
as well, and to the person
who takes your cloak, do not
withhold even your tunic.
Give to everyone who asks..."

I made the Sign of the Cross
on myself at these words of Jesus.

The revolution. From God.
The revolution of love from Jesus.

I believe in Jesus Christ. I believe.
But I have such difficulty loving.

I walked slowly to the seventh window:
in the Garden of Gethsemane
Jesus on his knees.

I made the Sign of the Cross
and opened the Holy Bible.
I whispered in the silence:

"Then Jesus came with them to
a place called Gethsemane, and
he said to his disciples: 'Sit here
while I go over there and pray.
My father, if it is possible, let
this cup pass from me; yet, not
as I will, but as You will.' When
He returned, the disciples were asleep."

I crossed myself.

I believe that Jesus is the son of God,
sent to redeem us from sin.
Have mercy on me, Father.

Jesus, save me from sin and death.

The eighth window: Jesus Crucified.

Nailed to the wood cross with thieves.
Jesus of Nazareth, King of the Jews.
Humiliated by the world.

I kneeled, whispered from the Holy Bible:

"And when they came to a place
called Golgotha (which means
Place of the Skull), they gave
Jesus wine to drink mixed with
gall. But when He tasted it, He
refused to drink. After they had

crucified Him, they divided
His garments by casting lots.; then
they sat down and kept watch
over Him there. And they placed
over His head the written charge
against Him: This is Jesus,
King of the Jews."

I felt the sorrow in myself.

*As in the Garden of Eden, man
defiant of God.*

*God, have mercy on me: I have
crucified your Son. Jesus,
save me from temptation and sin.
Save me from the death I have created.*

I walked slowly to the ninth window:
Jesus leaving the tomb, Jesus
Rising from the Grave.

*I do believe Jesus was resurrected
from death by God. I believe.*

I knelt before the window
and made the Sign of the Cross
on myself in the silence.

*I have been freed from death
through the love of God,
through the love of Jesus, who
conquered death, obedient to God.*

The tenth window: Jesus appearing
to the Disciples on the road to Emmaus
after His Resurrection.

I kneeled in the aisle before the appearance
of Jesus to the disciples. I crossed myself.

I emptied myself before Jesus.

*I believe. I believe Jesus is with God,
having shown us the way to life
everlasting. To freedom.*

Jesus is risen. Jesus is living.

*I believe Jesus conquered
sin and death, chaos and darkness.*

*I believe Jesus is the son of God.
I believe. I am alive.*

I knelt in silence.

last word

<pre>
                                    tired

         not   much   to   see
                                              i   know

                   no   more   writing
    last   words   in   thought   my   mind
                                   no   more   words   on   paper
         no   pencil   no   pen
                        no   computer   typing
              no   real   words
                                        i   cant   speak   to   her
    i   see   her
                        no   words   cant
         what   would   i   write

                                         tired
                                              last   words
         speak   last
                        think   cant   speak
                                         cant   write
         what   would   i   write
                                    she   is   there

                             and   tom   tom   too
              feel   nothing
                                         last   words   to
         what   words   would   i
                        write   in   my   mind   words
</pre>

one   word

                 i   think

                                love

   one   word

        four   four   letters   one   word

  im   writing   in   my   mind

                  can   you   see   the   word

                               speak

can   you   hear

                its   not   much

                                   not   long

  the   word

               love

                    remember   will   you

                  tired   just   the   word

      sleep

                           last   word   one

where   are   you

                      you   hear   me

no   more   words

                            where

     i   dont   see

                   dont   feel

  love

thats   what   i   to   write

cant

          think

                    hear   me

hear

She held his hand.

His fingers were cool.

Self-portrait

Rembrandt painted
himself

in the eyes of God.

E

Native Sone

a personal poem

her freckles, her color,
her warmth,
was a surprise
to him
in the twilight –

a young woman standing behind a car
in the street –

he'd been reluctant
to meet the stranger –

he learned her name –

and he met her the next afternoon –

in the sun light,
her freckles,
her color, radiated a heat –

he was creating with words
when he met her, unsettled, angry –

they talked through the afternoon –

and he met her
the next afternoon –

they talked –

she enveloped him in her warmth
as she talked quietly,
and laughed quietly –

she was real –

her face
freckled light brown, skin
with an orange glow,
pink
brushed on her cheeks,
a blue vein
at her temple –

she was alive laughing quietly –

Jacqueline –

she was love –

she is warm –

Interkourse

Senselessness,
is
    normal,
    reigns
            in the   woods
            be-
            hinde
                the house –
                        and
  as
      much
          in
            human
                  lyfe –
            so
that,
iff
    diatoms
          exist
          in
            their
           multifariety, so
            too
                dolphins'   intelligense,
there
      is   another form
          ov
           langwidge
                we, humann
              beings,

can

yuse:

it

isn't

any-

morr

senselesse   than   *thiss,*

the

new/thing!

forr

like/the

diatom – it

is

perfektlie

naturral!

a new

langwidge .

with lyfe's

senselessnesse

(realyzed)

from the wylde woods.

fertilyzashun!UP!

UP   from the mud-

earth,

urth

VITALYZASHUN

WITH

(imperfekshun). . .

grene.

2.

Dif/rens/
ex
  ists,
       so—
       in
            tha nu
            langwidge,
               much
               iznt
                   lefft owt
                   ov
                            lyfe"
ringenge,,
               in&owt

       (diatoma –)
                   spidrs,flowrs.

                   behind
                   tha – howss

               neer
       enunsia-
       teng

                    cleerlie

                dif/renz/z . . .

                        in,ov/

                              FORM –

  in   there.   arr

                            treez.

                        leav/z!

            (aer–)

                            smal

                            gren

                            leav/z !

                              burch/z

  a

    Birde

        dropt

            from   owt/ov

            tha spas:

        & tha gra

        kat

                watchez,wates
                withh
                    tha burd –
              WATES

crouch/z ,
         chargez!
          akros   the gren
            grasss
                        catcheng   it!
                    "killeng   it!
                      Qwikee: its
              its
                  flite, jusik
                    ded

    (in tha katz)

    mowthe–)

                        beaz on
                          dandely/onz

NOW   contin
    uus-
        lee
                moveng . .
                            . . (yello
                                yello
                                yello!
                                              kat

    (YELLO!

          2 leggs,

              no-
                    tail,and,

                                             an

                                                     'eye:)

              Beyutifull   katt–

                              on

                                      "   tha   blu   lawne,   "
                                      be-
                                      sid

                                              tha red

                                        red ,   treaz.

                                             (*oh!*)

              –tha gra

                   dandelyon/z,

                              200 ft,

                                     TALLE

              FLYENG   AROUNDE

                      tha   kat yello –

       danseng,danseng   *nise.*
                                               lie . . .

                                        . . NOW

                      sekshual
                            inter

kours

,*withh*

(FLOWRZ:)?

" no idears but

in   thengs . . dandy LIONZ!YESS!*YESS!* "

inter,kourse .

Yes sir.

Death is near

I will burn these white birches,
    into my mind;
I will burn the birds' piping song,
    into my mind;
I will burn these moving white clouds,
    into my mind;
I will burn her orange and freckled face,
    deep into my mind.
For death is near. Death is coming.

Softening the line

For JTF

The man looked at her body naked
in front of him.

Her eyes moved
as he moved slowly to her left.

He stopped, looked at her body,
his hand covering his mouth,
elbow resting on his forearm at his waist.

He was not naked.
He looked at the line of her naked shoulder
moving along her arm to her forearm to her hand
at her hip.

His eyes rested momentarily
on her pubic hair,
chestnut colored.

He turned away from the woman, his hand
still covering his mouth.
He walked slowly to his left,
stopped, turned to face the woman.

He stood directly
in front of her, looked at her shoulders,
the slight recesses at her collar bones, then
down to her breasts, looking
at both.

They were round, with good sized aureoles.

She watched him, not moving.

The man's eyes moved slowly over her breasts,
then to the woman's navel,
over the slight rise of her stomach,
to her pubic hair.

He turned his head to the right and looked at her body
with his left eye,
narrowing his eye, seeing
from her navel across her stomach
to her hip, her arm resting almost
on the crest.

He turned around, his back to the woman.

He stood for a moment, then
turned back, looking at the woman's face,
quickly looking down her body to her feet.

The woman was freckled, with chestnut colored hair, her body resonant
with orange light.

He stared at her.

Then, he turned slowly
to his left, picked up the brush, and made a red line
on the canvas, slowly
a long, undulant line.

He looked at the woman's naked body.

The man then thickened the line with orange, muting
the harshness of the red, adding an ochre to the orange, softening
the edge of the line.

He looked at the woman naked. He could see the line vibrating
with an orange light like fire.

He stood away from the canvas,
backed up, then
looked at the woman.

He stared at her.

He could see fire.

He stood away from the naked woman,
his hand covering his eyes.

He could see life.

creation now a roar

Unlike the neat black typed words of poetry on white paper creation now
is a continually hot and bloody and violent and painful
action,
devastating
and liberating simultaneously, a roar.

Noland

Note: Noland is a five part book length piece.

An island off the Pacific coast

My name is John.

I never thought life
would end this way for me.

I began to search
 for an answer
   the day I woke
    from death.
        I thought I was condemned
         if I didn't find
          the answer.

And I became a fugitive,
      death trailing me.

I began
 the year of Apollo XIII,
   the year Charles De Gaulle died,
    when the film *Love Story* packed the theaters
   and Viet Nam student protesters were killed at Kent State
      by the national guard.

But those events pale in my memory now.

My name is John Rollins.

I've been drifting the country
 for twenty nine years.

  I was thirty-six years old when
 my life turned inside out.

At the time,
 everything was going as it should.
  I was vice president of a big textile company,
    based at a mill in a small Maine city.
I lived in a hundred thousand dollar century old home with my wife, Evelyn,
    and my two sons, with a pool, camp, a Volvo
      a BMW, the works.

Alan, my oldest son, was working for GM, and

my youngest son, Ed, was in college,
at Yale.

I was living the American dream.

The dream of all people actually.

I was Alan Tippens:
J. Alan Tippens, Vice President.
My name is John Rollins now.

I'd just vacationed with Evelyn
on the Maine coastal island where her mother had been born.

I remember the sun shining through the bathroom window
the day after we arrived home from vacation.
I was looking at my face in the mirror.

Then I heard Evelyn's voice calling me
from far away.
I woke
and she was trying to lift me off the floor.

I spent six days in the hospital.
because I was bleeding internally,

I had no idea what had happened. I remembered nothing.

Two weeks after I left the hospital,
I passed out again, this time in my backyard.
I spent a week in bed at home then.

I went back to work finally, but
I wasn't able to concentrate.

I'd catch myself
standing at the window,
looking out, looking
at nothing.

I felt sometimes that my mind was a blank,
as if something had been erased.

At other times, I felt an irrational fear come into me.
Suddenly it came, and suddenly it would disappear.

I began to neglect my vegetable garden at home.
I loved to work in the garden, down
on my knees, in the dirt.

But suddenly
I just didn't care.

I stopped washing the cars. I'd washed the two cars
every third day of my adult life without fail.

They were a real satisfaction in my life.
I'd always traded cars every two years.

I felt nothing for the cars.

I began to turn my chair to the window
at work, and sit,
staring out the window.

Still looking at nothing.
I didn't work. I didn't even pass the work on to someone else.

As time passed, I began to feel that my mind was shifting between reality
and unreality.
The blankness
in my mind, a sudden irrational fear, and then unreality.
My mind seemed unbalanced.

It was unnerving because I couldn't control it.
And I didn't understand it.
I began to cry one day when I was sitting at the window staring at nothing.

When I stopped crying, I left the office.

I never returned. I never
offered an explanation to the company and
refused to communicate about it.

I sat around in the eleven room century-old house and did nothing.

I sat in the backyard for hours.

Evelyn was in shock. And the boys were mystified by my behavior.

But they were as mystified by my behavior as I was. I did not know
what was happening.

They had all felt that I would need time to recuperate
after the internal bleeding incident, but this was not the recuperation
they or anyone understood.

I refused to talk about it with Evelyn
or the boys.

My business associates came to the house,
but I got rid of them without explanation.

The company fired me.
I wasn't concerned.

I continued to sit in the backyard.

I felt as if I had lost control of my life.
And I really didn't care.

That was what was so mystifying.

I began to have a dream.
I was locked outside a house, alone, looking inside.
It was dark, black, outside the house.
The house was made of glass.
A light shone inside the rooms of the house.
The light quivered. The house looked like my house.
But I was not certain that it was my house. It was glass.
I was afraid in the dream
because I was locked outside. I was afraid to be locked out in the dark.

I was shouting for someone to let me in,
but I couldn't hear the sound from my shouting.

I was pounding on the glass walls, but
there was no sound from my hitting the glass.
I usually woke from the dream as I was shouting and pounding soundlessly
in a panic.
I felt very much alone.

This dream returned often, among other dreams less fearful.
I felt this dream was a threat, a warning, to me.
But I didn't know why it was.

I grew a beard, let my hair grow long. I lost weight
because I ate without interest.
Food had lost its delight for me.
And I looked older than my age. I looked old.

I was not interested in anything.

Then the idea began to grow in my mind
that I no longer knew the answers to life.
The answers
I once knew, which helped me live every day without question,
seemed to have disappeared.

I began to feel insecure in life.

My mind
was still shifting between the real
and the unreal. And the irrational fear would come.
Then the dream.

I began to fill small pocket notebooks with questions
about life, and society.

The questions were often nonsense,
in an illegible scrawl.

I ignored my beloved dog, Sheena.
The dog had always been a faithful companion.

Evelyn goaded me every day.

I wasn't concerned.
I didn't care. Rather,
I couldn't care. And I didn't know why.

I wasn't interested in her,
or the boys.

One morning, I had a short dream.
I dreamed that I was locked inside the glass house, not
outside as I usually was. But I was shouting and pounding,
this time to get outside.
The glass house disappeared and
I was falling through the blackness of space, out of control.

I woke with a terrible fear.

I was shaken to the depths of my soul by this dream,
waking in the unfathomable darkness, free falling, clear in my mind.

I left home that day.
I disappeared.

I ran.
I was afraid.

I walked out of the house without saying goodbye to Evelyn.

It was too late for explanations. And I didn't want to offer her one.

I took nothing with me.

I left my wallet on the coffee table and walked out the door.

I left my hundred thousand dollar home, swimming pool, the camp, cars, and
all the other accumulated goods I'd worked so hard for.

And I left my beloved dog.

On that morning I suddenly knew something that I had not known before.

I knew that one morning I'd died.
My life had been snuffed out against my will. And
I had not seen God, wherever it was I went.

I had seen nothing.

I had been in the blackness of space.

I was afraid.
I left the house with death literally trailing me.

I felt death behind me.

I've drifted around the country.

I've worked in restaurants as a dishwasher or short order cook,
on garbage trucks or at other jobs like that, for food and a roof over my head.

I changed my name to John Rollins.
An undistinctive name, easy to forget.

J. Alan Tippens was gone.

I kept out of sight in case Evelyn or the boys
decided I was worth searching for.

I never tried to contact the family.

When I would dream of the glass house, ending now with the blackness of space and my free fall,
the terrible fear engulfing me,
I would move on from wherever I happened to be.
No one
missed me because I was just passing through.

I was afraid.

I was a lost soul.

I'm in a village now, on the Pacific coast.
It's an old village which has seen better days.
Most of the people here are old, retired fishing people.

I understand there used to be a tourist
season. Not any more.

I clean up yards, chop wood, general handyman around the village for the older people.

I live in a boarding house with a hundred year old woman
as landlady.

I won't leave the island. The drifting, the running, is done. It's over.

Death is here with me.

John Rollins is here. No one is here.

On the Bridge

On the Williamsburg Bridge

Sonny Rollins
gold horn
singing joy,
singing hope,
black man
with gold horn
high
in the air,
circling,
flying
sound
in the air.

Untitled 827

to watch   to be   she is here   sitting up

sitting   in   bed   sun   the window beside the bed
              in the window   the window beside her
                                                    and, sun is
coming in the window
                                    her hand moves as she speaks   speaking
                              she moves
        slowly   in   bed
                                                              in the sun light
                                                                            animated, she is
        with the sun light   but she does not stand
                                          and speaking, she smiles
                    she did walk   she does not walk
                                                        lying in the bed
                                                                                room unfamiliar
                                          she is familiar
            it is not unexpected   she is speaking, moving her hand, gesturing, smiling

        the window is clean and the sun shines through the window into the room

and the sun is shining this afternoon on the trees   in to the room

                                    he is sitting in the chair next to the bed
                  next to her
                                                                                sun warm on his shoulders
                                                        through the window
        watching her   listening, to her   to her words
                                                                                the room is warm
                                                    (she is hopeful
            and it is the first time she is sitting
                                                                the sun is yellow warm
            a yellow color
                                                the room is open   even unfamiliar
                                                                        the room is not dark
        (another time   rain falling and the room was dark
                                                                she smiles
              and he laughs then
                                                                            (there is not much pain now
                  she has forgotten the past three days
                                                            sitting in the sun light
                                                                        (agony
        she smiles and her face colors   she relaxes, smiling

                                        the man sees the light orange color in the woman's face then

                                                                            (he hopes

                  the sun is hot on his back

    with the sun light in the room   she is open   she is full,

                                                and it is warm

Native Sone

Malcolm Robbins, born and raised in Rockland Maine, was convicted of sexually molesting a murdering a boy in Santa Barbara, California. He molested and killed an 8 year old boy in New Jersey and also murdered a 17 year old in West Virginia.

Rockland, – at
the coast,
ferry
       to islands
Lobster Festival
& Farnsworth, the
Wyeths
       nearby in
Cushing – Owls Head:
antique cars,
planes,
Camden w / Millay

writing verses as

a child
Maine – Rockland –
native
       Malcolm Rollins,
Mackey, "Mickey Mouse"
Big ears, Dumbo

native to Maine,
Rockland (b 1959).
sone

borderLine IQ
Slow walker
       dirtY
apartment=Mother,
welfare child:

Mackey, sister-Mom

    19.
WelfARe

Mickey Mouse expelled
from kindergarten –

Mom / 8th grade:
          uncles

beat
kid
            unfathered,

6; 6,
                . . raped
                            by
    1
            ov mothers frends..
a
man.. .
littl
                boy —
:(garbage in corner).

to Camden, Millays,
fields, ocean,
forest
            sky wide,
writing,

<u>smart girl</u>

<u>raped at six Mackey</u>

11: poisoned
                        his
3 yr / old
                cousin
(often alone
                    on
  Rockland streets
&
  Moms brothers
incarcerated

4
  violence)!so?

<u>Me / Youth Ctr / 11</u>

11"?danger
      to society"
11-18,in&
                out of
(leave; sex
  ual assaults) —

Maine has a long irregular coast with fine
beaches and harbors that attract many tourists
& summer residents Old Orchard Beach
Boothbay Harbor Camden & Bar Harbor are

some of the better known resorts
                & Louise Nevelson in
Rockland as child: <u>Black</u>

    <u>Wall</u>
            construktion

    <u>Mickey Mouse</u> in Portland w / his
    mother - 4th grade - burned his
    school papers trying to burn the
    classroom. One day, his pet cat
    scratched him so he strangled it
    hanged it on the clothesline and
            set it afire.
            Doc (shrink) "prognosis
    for this boy w / out some institu
    tional intervention is poor. The boys
    potential for violence and further
    deterioration is great.
                Dumbo's 3 yr old cousin
    ruined a football game so
    he put Lysol in
                Kool-Aid bottle
    cousin drank it / stomach pumped
    psychologist at Boys Training Center
    recommended counseling
                        on a regular
    long-term basis   :none
                    given

    Mackey, scruffy kid, pulling
    pocket knife
                on streets
                    , alone
            (transfer:Childrens Psychiatric
            Pownal / 9 mos / no
                continuous treat. . .

    return'd to Mom / four husbands
        in Rockland, home / birth
            place
            of Millay
                    BACK TO
            TRAINING CTR: chased
                2 kids - "cut yr throats!"
            assaulted 6 yr old boy?

    11/ 20 / 1974
                wedged toothbrush
            in vent
                    .white sheet

around neck (14) Hangeng!

        almost made it . . . . . . ,
            medicine: thorazine,stelazine))
        spring 1975,
                        to Moms,care
                        @ 5 mos sex-
                            assalt-3-yr-
                        Old
    Mom's / men / frends: sexual / forseng
                - Court:cop / "Sexual
                                deviate
        will
    probly admit this / assaltd himself)
        probably can't reason
            this is very wrong"

the ferry for Vinalhaven leaves Rockland at 3 PM from pier

                psychologist endorsed Mackey
            Mouse request to go
            Bangor Mental Health Insti-
still @ BTC:
    3 Doc's contacts / 74
    3   "   "   / 75   (uncommitted to BMHI
    3   "   "   / 76   by judge)
        not treated at Me Medical /   Portland . . . .

                    "MM" requested treat;
                    psychs notes / no
                            recommendation...

            GRANTED
                LEAVE
            "feels must strike"
            "cannot stabilize"

                        16

                         s

                         O

                         d

                         o

                         m

                         y

        6 y e a r   o l d

                         Maine b   o y   –

received wkly visits / on lv in Scarborough-uncle / by psychologists
            "DANGER G E R "   -18   10/12/78-
                                        discharged   )))

  d   r
               i   f   ,t
                                      U.   S   .
                                 w /

                ol   d   ' r   h   o   mo   's
                              :Santa   Barbara
                         C   alifForNI,A   ,
(@18,where was
            Millay?
      in beautiful

                         Camden, Maine, just
              north,   on   the   coast,   of   her
                   birthplace,
                      Rockland   -
                         written
                            "Renascence"
                              rebirth
                                    of a native))

        M A C K E Y   T O O K   6 YR   O L D D   B O Y   F O R   A
M O T O R C Y C L E   R I   D   E   T W IS   T   E D
        T HE
                    C   H I   L   D   !N   E C   K

                         , the trial

              1   9   8   0   s   t   a   B

                 9 (yr)   o

                                    b   y
)NJ.)
                                              sE   !x

              west Vr   g   n a
                    1 7   yr
                         K I!L! L! -!

                    —— / charged   12:79   sodomy
                                              6 yr: DalaS-81

                                                                        80
                              stABB   15/boy

                                                              black wall,

        disbelief/MiLlAy, roC   k.l
                                        a n /d

                                                        MAINE

                                        native
                                        with
    (((on the   edg   e   .,   ,

                    Lobster Festival - August -

                        "all the lobsters
                            from   the   Maine
                                sea
                                          you can
                                eat!"
                            se
                                                          .x ,

            littl boy
              littl boy   native

                    , m a n .

        Edna St. Vincent Millay was at Vassar College @   at   23
                                                        native Maineiac Millay & Mackey

                    (to be continued)

Desire

*When you wake from sleep, repeat the following phrase until you are exhausted.
Do not stop no matter what your activity is. If your activity forces you to stop
repeating the phrase, stop the activity. Continue to repeat the phrase until you
can no longer repeat the phrase, until you are exhausted.*

I am destructive and creative.

Listening to the birds

You like the birds,
      he asked, hesitant.

Yes. Do you, she asked,
          hesitating.

I walk in the woods, he said.

She didn't say anything.
      She bent her neck.

We could go now. If you want,
      he said.

She raised her head, looked
      into his eyes.

We don't have to, no, he said,
     thinking he had overstepped.

We could, If you want,
      she answered. I guess.

I have a place where cardinals
      meet, he said. And other birds.

I usually don't walk In the woods,
      she said. Alone.

I don't know, I like to get away,
     I guess, he said, as they walked.

I walk along the road for birds,
     and flowers, wildflowers, she said.

Listen, he touched his finger to her arm.
     There it is, he said quietly.

They stopped.

The cardinal
     was squeezing out his liquid whistles.

There he is, he said, quietly,
         Looking at her.

I can't see him, she said,
     looking into the trees for the bird.

Let's go slow, we'll find him,
                he said to her.

They walked together slowly toward
        the cardinal's song.

He put his hand on her arm and
                stopped. She stopped.

They both listened. The cardinal
        was high above them in a great maple.

She turned and smiled to him.
                That's it, she said.

You do like birds,
        he whispered.

Yes, she whispered.
                I told you I did.

Listen, the other one, that's the female,
        answering him, he whispered.

I hear it, yes, she smiled. Over there.

He smiled as the bird whistles passed
        from one tree to the other.

They stood together, listening.

From the corner of his eye
        he saw her concentration.

He touched her arm with his finger,
        whispering, You hear them?

Yes, she whispered, but
                I still don't see them.

The singing is beautiful, he whispered.

Yes, she murmured, listening intently.

The two birds whistled in the trees
        over their heads.

There was no other sound in the woods.

His finger touched her arm and
        she touched his finger.

He closed his eyes and bent his neck.

Close your eyes, he said, and listen.

She closed her eyes. Listened.
          She bent her neck to listen.

They listened to the two birds
          calling back and forth.

Do you believe in God,
          he whispered to her.

She opened her eyes to look at him.
          His eyes were closed.

She didn't answer.

Listen, he whispered, his words
                    almost inaudible.

She listened.

She closed her eyes.

She heard his breath.

Blood on sweet lips

From Edna St. Vincent Millay

She would sleep with anyone she pleased,
man or woman, holding feverishly to her body
as to a god, her words moving as quickly
as her hand injecting morphine into her thigh
to stop the pain, her soul imprisoned in the sky.
She died by her own hand, blood on sweet lips.

Tom Fallon

subtitled his first book, "Selected Poems, Half-poems and Non-poems," in 1978, clearly establishing his direction for exploring poetry and literary form rather than following inherited poetry forms. How to write, has been his primary question, opening up his mind to creation. Fallon's subsequent books, "Pregnant Man 1" in *Red Dust 3, The Man on the Moon*, continued exploration and invention of form to the point where he posited a new literary term, charteng, after discovering Marianne Moore's statement in an interview with Donald Hall for the Paris Review: "What I write, as I have said before, is only called poetry because there is no other category." This term relates to the new categories in the fine arts such as collage, environments, etc. Fallon's creation was first affected by exposure to modern painting in his youth, then modern jazz, experimental classical music, happenings and Off-Off Broadway theater of New York in the Seventies. His use of the whole space of the 8 1/2 and larger spaced page, the wall writings, relates to his original visual or fine art direction as a youth. The thinking and writings of William Carlos Williams is the primary literary influence on his work.

Order the Wall Writings

The purchaser of NOW may order the wall writings by sending a postcard to the author at the following address. The creations will be sent without charge.

Tom Fallon
Wall Writings
239 Spruce St.
Rumford ME 04276-2250

The wall writings are a recent extension of many years' exploration of word lines, line and space, the total space, of the 8 1/2 x 11 inch page.

The writings are of any size, from less than 8 1/2 x 11 to 2' x 3' or larger. In the 2' x 3' and larger sizes, space is a more significant factor than it is in the smaller sizes. Also, multiple pages have been used for a single creation. The wall itself can be a factor.

The wall writings are meant to be placed on a wall to be viewed. They are meant to be "lived with as they exist on the wall." They are not meant to be held in the hand or read aloud. Yes, one might read them aloud spontaneously (as they exist on the wall) if that seems appropriate at any time. The point for reading aloud is that there should be no restrictions on the viewer or reader for exploring the writings.

The wall writings are meant to be viewed, encompassed, on the wall.